EASY CHICKEN DISHES

The following Canadian companies were involved in the production
of this Collection: Colour Technologies, Fred Bird & Associates Limited,
Gordon Sibley Design Inc., On-line Graphics, Telemedia Publishing Inc. and
The Madison Book Group Inc.

We acknowledge the contribution of
Drew Warner, Joie Warner and Flavor Publications.

Produced by
The Madison Book Group Inc.
40 Madison Avenue
Toronto, Ontario
Canada
M5R 2S1

EASY CHICKEN DISHES

■ *On our cover: Chicken with Pasta and Peppers (p. 53)*

Chicken — what would we do without it! It's tasty, versatile and a hands-down family favorite. But if you sometimes wonder about new ways to cook it, we have over 50 different and delicious answers for you! Slice it into hearty *Chicken Caesar Sandwiches* or *Skillet Chicken Salad*. Spice it up in tangy *Hoisin Wings* or *Jamaican Jerked Chicken*. Barbecue it in *Pesto Chicken Burgers* or *Honey-Citrus Chicken Kabobs*. Or dress it up for dinner in hearty *Chicken Cacciatore with Artichokes* or elegant *Chicken Paella*. Whatever the occasion or the season, here are a wealth of easy and inexpensive year-round recipes for chicken and turkey — plus handy shopping and cooking tips and microwave shortcuts.

Easy Chicken Dishes is just one of the eight full-color cookbooks that make up THE CANADIAN LIVING COOKING COLLECTION. Inside each of these colorful cookbooks are the kind of satisfying, easy-to-make dishes you'll want to cook over and over again. Each recipe in the Collection has been carefully selected and tested by *Canadian Living* to make sure it turns out wonderfully every time you make it. When you collect all eight cookbooks, you can choose from over 500 dishes — from marvelous soups to sensational desserts — all guaranteed to make any meal extra special.

Elizabeth Baird

Elizabeth Baird
Food Director, *Canadian Living* Magazine

Chicken Caesar Sandwiches

Instead of cooked chicken, you can use smoked chicken or turkey. For our photograph, we made a king-size sandwich.

1/2 lb	**bacon**	**250 g**
2	**tomatoes, halved, seeded and diced**	**2**
1 lb	**cooked chicken breasts, diced**	**500 g**
4 cups	**coarsely chopped romaine lettuce**	**1 L**
16	**slices French bread**	**16**
	DRESSING	
1	**clove garlic, minced**	**1**
2 tbsp	**red wine vinegar**	**25 mL**
1 tbsp	**anchovy paste**	**15 mL**
1 tbsp	**lemon juice**	**15 mL**
1 tbsp	**Dijon mustard**	**15 mL**
1/3 cup	**olive oil**	**75 mL**
3 tbsp	**mayonnaise**	**50 mL**
3 tbsp	**freshly grated Parmesan cheese**	**50 mL**
1 tsp	**Worcestershire sauce**	**5 mL**
Pinch	**cayenne pepper**	**Pinch**
	Salt and pepper	

■ In skillet, cook bacon over medium heat for about 4 minutes or until crisp. Drain on paper towel; break into 1/2-inch (1 cm) pieces. Drain tomatoes well; combine with bacon and chicken.

■ **Dressing:** In large bowl, combine garlic, vinegar, anchovy paste, lemon juice and mustard. Whisk in oil, then mayonnaise; stir in cheese, Worcestershire sauce, cayenne, and salt and pepper to taste. (Don't worry if mixture separates; it will still work well.)

■ Toss chicken mixture with dressing. Marinate in refrigerator for at least 30 minutes or up to 4 hours. Just before assembling sandwiches, add lettuce. Sandwich between bread. Makes 8 sandwiches.

Hoisin Wings

Hoisin chicken wings are a treat served either hot or cold. For a picnic, be sure to chill the chicken wings before packing into the cooler.

1/3 cup	**hoisin sauce**	**75 mL**
1/4 cup	**ketchup**	**50 mL**
1/4 cup	**liquid honey**	**50 mL**
1 tsp	**grated orange rind**	**5 mL**
2 tbsp	**orange juice**	**25 mL**
1 tbsp	**Dijon mustard**	**15 mL**
2 tsp	**minced gingerroot**	**10 mL**
2 tsp	**Worcestershire sauce**	**10 mL**
2	**cloves garlic, minced**	**2**
1/4 tsp	**cayenne pepper**	**1 mL**
3 lb	**chicken wings**	**1.5 kg**

■ In large bowl, combine hoisin sauce, ketchup, honey, orange rind and juice, mustard, gingerroot, Worcestershire sauce, garlic and cayenne.

■ Remove tips from wings; separate wings at joint. Add wings to sauce and toss to coat. Remove wings, shaking off and reserving excess sauce; arrange in single layer on greased foil-lined baking sheet. Bake in 400°F (200°C) oven for 15 minutes. Brush with remaining sauce and bake, turning and basting at least twice, for about 40 minutes longer or until no longer pink inside and deep brown on outside. Makes about 6 servings.

Lemon-Rosemary Chicken Wings

Serve hot with drinks or nibble on these succulent wings cold as a midnight or noon-hour snack.

2 lb	**chicken wings**	**1 kg**
2 tbsp	**olive oil**	**25 mL**
2 tbsp	**lemon juice**	**25 mL**
1 tbsp	**grated lemon rind**	**15 mL**
2	**cloves garlic, minced**	**2**
1 tsp	**dried rosemary**	**5 mL**
1/2 tsp	**each salt and pepper**	**2 mL**

■ Remove tips from wings; reserve for stock. Separate wings at joint. Place in bowl just big enough to hold wings.

■ In small saucepan, stir together oil, lemon juice, lemon rind, garlic, rosemary, salt and pepper; simmer over medium-low heat for 10 minutes. Pour over wings and toss to coat; marinate for 30 minutes at room temperature or for up to 8 hours in refrigerator (bring to room temperature before continuing).

■ Arrange wings in single layer in shallow pan; bake, uncovered, in 425°F (220°C) oven for 20 to 25 minutes or until golden brown and no longer pink inside. Makes about 2 dozen.

WING IT!
Chicken wings are as irresistible as peanuts — you can never eat just one! Economical, fast and easy, wings are perfect as a main course, as tasty snacks for casual entertaining or for portable lunches. These tasty morsels are a cut above all other finger foods.

- *When purchasing chicken wings, buy the freshest ones available. Fresh chicken wings should have smooth skins and no odors.*
- *In our recipes, we suggest trimming the wing tips (reserve for making stock) and separating the wings into sections. This is optional but it ensures even cooking.*

Creole Chicken Wings with Peach Mustard Sauce

These spicy wings will be a hit with everyone. Cooked at an unusually high temperature, the chicken is crusty on the outside, tender and juicy within.

3 lb	**chicken wings**	**1.5 kg**
4	**cloves garlic, minced**	**4**
2 tsp	**each dry mustard and paprika**	**10 mL**
1 tsp	**each dried thyme and granulated sugar**	**5 mL**
1/2 tsp	**each cayenne pepper, salt and black pepper**	**2 mL**
1/4 cup	**lemon juice**	**50 mL**
	PEACH MUSTARD SAUCE	
1/2 cup	**peach jam**	**125 mL**
1 tbsp	**Dijon mustard**	**15 mL**
2 tsp	**diced pimiento**	**10 mL**
1 tsp	**cider vinegar**	**5 mL**

■ Cut tips off wings; reserve for stock. In small bowl, stir together garlic, mustard, paprika, thyme, sugar, cayenne, salt and black pepper; blend in lemon juice to make paste.

■ Using pastry brush, brush paste over wings. Arrange wings, meaty side down, on lightly greased foil-lined baking sheets. Let stand for 30 minutes at room temperature.

■ Bake in 475°F (240°C) oven for 15 minutes; turn wings over and bake for 15 to 20 minutes or until brown, crisp and no longer pink inside.

■ **Peach Mustard Sauce:** In saucepan, melt jam over low heat; stir in mustard, pimiento and vinegar. Pass separately for dipping. Makes 4 main-course or 8 appetizer servings.

Pesto Chicken Burgers

These chicken burgers with their summery pesto flavors — basil, pine nuts and cheese — are delicious served on 4-inch (10 cm) lengths of toasted French bread (baguette).

1	**egg**	**1**
1/4 cup	**bread crumbs**	**50 mL**
3 tbsp	**water or chicken stock**	**50 mL**
2 tbsp	**chopped fresh basil**	**25 mL**
2 tbsp	**chopped green onion**	**25 mL**
2 tbsp	**freshly grated Parmesan cheese**	**25 mL**
1 tbsp	**pine nuts or slivered almonds**	**15 mL**
1/2 tsp	**salt**	**2 mL**
1/4 tsp	**pepper**	**1 mL**
1 lb	**ground chicken**	**500 g**

■ In bowl, beat egg; mix in bread crumbs, water, basil, onion, Parmesan, pine nuts, salt and pepper. Blend in chicken; shape into 4 patties.

■ Place patties on greased grill over medium-hot coals or at medium-high setting; barbecue for 5 minutes. Turn and cook for about 7 minutes or until no longer pink inside. Makes 4 servings.

CHICKEN BURGERS INSTEAD

Chicken burgers are a nice change from hamburgers and contain much less fat. More and more supermarkets feature ground chicken and even turkey. If you have a food processor, you can grind skinless, boneless chicken breasts yourself; if not, ask the butcher to do it for you. Once the chicken is ground, use it within a day because ground meat spoils easily.

Herbed Chicken Burgers with Lemon Sauce

Serve these tasty burgers with sautéed zucchini and carrots.

1 lb	**chicken breasts, skinned and boned**	**500 g**
1 cup	**fresh bread crumbs**	**250 mL**
1/2 cup	**plain yogurt**	**125 mL**
1	**egg**	**1**
1/3 cup	**chopped fresh parsley**	**75 mL**
1-1/2 tsp	**salt**	**7 mL**
1 tsp	**each dried tarragon and chervil**	**5 mL**
1/2 tsp	**dried thyme**	**2 mL**
1/2 tsp	**pepper**	**2 mL**
3 tbsp	**unsalted butter**	**50 mL**
1/2 cup	**dry white wine**	**125 mL**
1/4 cup	**lemon juice**	**50 mL**

■ Cut chicken into cubes and pat dry; process in food processor until ground. If chicken is already ground, place in large bowl.

■ Combine bread crumbs with yogurt; let stand for a few minutes.

■ In bowl, combine chicken, yogurt mixture and egg. Add 2 tbsp (25 mL) of the parsley, salt, tarragon, chervil, thyme and pepper; mix well. Shape into 6 large patties, about 1-1/2 inches (4 cm) thick.

■ In large skillet, heat butter over medium-high heat; cook patties for about 7 minutes on each side or until well browned and no longer pink inside. Remove to serving platter.

■ Pour off excess fat from pan. Add wine and lemon juice; bring to boil, stirring to scrape up browned bits from bottom of pan. Cook until reduced to about 1/4 cup (50 mL); add remaining parsley. Pour over burgers. Serve hot or cold. Makes 6 servings.

Skillet Chicken Salad

For a real change of pace, try this colorful hot salad — it's just the answer for a light supper.

4	**boneless skinless chicken breasts (about 1 lb/500 g)**	**4**
1	**sweet red pepper**	**1**
Half	**bunch broccoli (about 1/2 lb/250 g)**	**Half**
1/4 cup	**vegetable oil**	**50 mL**
1/4 cup	**chicken stock**	**50 mL**
3 tbsp	**vinegar**	**50 mL**
1 tbsp	**Dijon mustard**	**15 mL**
1 tsp	**dried tarragon**	**5 mL**
	Salt and pepper	
1 cup	**tiny whole mushrooms**	**250 mL**
2	**green onions, chopped**	**2**
	Boston or leaf lettuce	

■ Cut chicken crosswise into 1/2-inch (1 cm) wide strips. Seed and core red pepper; cut into strips. Cut broccoli into small florets; peel stalks and slice 1/4 inch (5 mm) thick.

■ In large skillet, heat 2 tbsp (25 mL) of the oil over medium heat; cook chicken, stirring occasionally, for about 4 minutes or until golden and no longer pink inside. Using slotted spoon, transfer chicken to warm bowl.

■ In same skillet, heat remaining oil; cook red pepper and broccoli for 2 minutes. Stir in stock and reduce heat to low; cover and steam for 2 minutes. Using slotted spoon, add red pepper and broccoli to chicken; cover to keep warm.

■ In same skillet, pour in vinegar; bring to boil, stirring to scrape up brown bits in pan. Stir in mustard, tarragon, and salt and pepper to taste. Add mushrooms and onions. Return chicken mixture and any accumulated juices to skillet; cook just to heat through. Serve on lettuce-lined dinner plates. Makes 4 servings.

Thai Orange Chicken Salad

A terrific flavor combination, this salad is great year-round. The dressing is mildly hot; if you like, increase the hot pepper flakes to 1 tsp (5 mL). If lettuce heads are small, use four.

2	large carrots	2
2	sweet red peppers	2
1 tsp	sesame oil	5 mL
3	green onions	3
2	cooked boneless skinless chicken breasts	2
2	heads Boston lettuce	2
1-1/2 cups	bean sprouts	375 mL
3/4 cup	fresh coriander	175 mL
2	oranges, halved and sliced	2

DRESSING

4	cloves garlic	4
2/3 cup	water	150 mL
1/2 cup	smooth peanut butter	125 mL
1/3 cup	rice vinegar	75 mL
1 tbsp	soy sauce	15 mL
1-1/2 tsp	granulated sugar	7 mL
1/2 tsp	crushed hot pepper flakes	2 mL

■ Using vegetable peeler, peel carrots into long strips. Seed and slice peppers into thin rounds. In nonstick skillet, heat oil over medium heat; cook carrots and red peppers for 5 minutes or until tender-crisp.

■ Leaving 1 inch (2.5 cm) of green at ends of onions, slice lengthwise into strips. Cut chicken into thin strips.

■ **Dressing:** In blender or food processor, chop garlic finely. Add water, peanut butter, vinegar, soy sauce, sugar and hot pepper flakes; process until smooth.

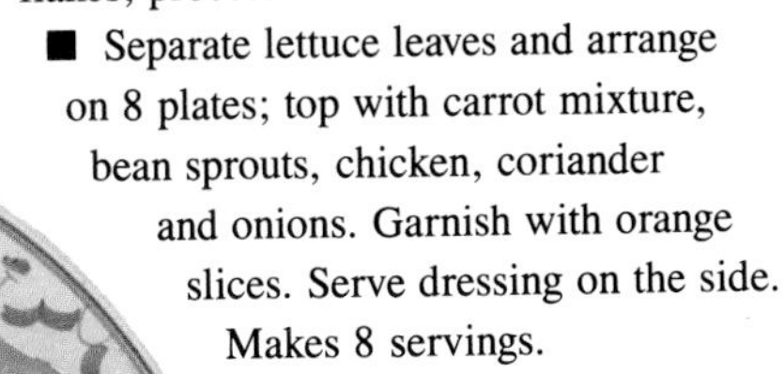

■ Separate lettuce leaves and arrange on 8 plates; top with carrot mixture, bean sprouts, chicken, coriander and onions. Garnish with orange slices. Serve dressing on the side. Makes 8 servings.

Layered Chicken Salad

This colorful salad stays crisp and delicious for up to one day.

4 cups	**torn spinach**	**1 L**
3 cups	**cubed cooked chicken or turkey**	**750 mL**
1	**small sweet red pepper, cut in thin rings**	**1**
4	**hard-cooked eggs, sliced**	**4**
	Salt and pepper	
Half	**English cucumber, thinly sliced**	**Half**
1 cup	**cooked macaroni (about 1/2 cup/125 mL uncooked)**	**250 mL**
1	**small red onion, thinly sliced**	**1**

	DRESSING	
3/4 cup	**mayonnaise**	**175 mL**
1/2 cup	**plain yogurt**	**125 mL**
1/4 cup	**finely chopped fresh parsley**	**50 mL**
1 tbsp	**granulated sugar**	**15 mL**
2 tsp	**finely chopped fresh dill (or 1/2 tsp/2 mL dried dillweed)**	**10 mL**

■ **Dressing:** Stir together mayonnaise, yogurt, 2 tbsp (25 mL) of the parsley, sugar and dill; set aside.

■ In straight-sided glass or plastic bowl, layer spinach, chicken, red pepper, eggs sprinkled with salt and pepper to taste, cucumber, macaroni and red onion, spreading evenly so edges of each layer are neat and visible.

■ Spoon dressing evenly over top. Garnish with remaining parsley. Cover tightly and refrigerate for several hours or overnight. Toss gently just before serving. Makes 6 to 8 servings.

Grilled Chicken and Cheese Salad

Barbecued chicken on simply dressed lettuce makes a quick warm salad.

1/3 cup	**olive oil**	**75 mL**
2 tbsp	**white wine vinegar**	**25 mL**
3/4 tsp	**each chopped fresh marjoram and sage (or 1/4 tsp/1 mL each dried)**	**4 mL**
1/2 tsp	**salt**	**2 mL**
1/4 tsp	**pepper**	**1 mL**
1 tbsp	**Dijon mustard**	**15 mL**
3	**boneless skinless chicken breasts**	**3**
6 cups	**mixed torn greens**	**1.5 L**
1 cup	**shredded Swiss cheese**	**250 mL**

■ Whisk together oil, vinegar, marjoram, sage, salt and pepper. In large bowl, combine 2 tbsp (25 mL) of the oil mixture with mustard. Add chicken, turning to coat all over.

■ Grill chicken on greased grill over medium-hot coals or at medium setting for 6 minutes per side or until no longer pink inside, turning once and brushing with any remaining mustard mixture.

■ Meanwhile, toss greens and cheese with remaining oil mixture; arrange on 4 plates. Cut cooked chicken into 1/2-inch (1 cm) thick strips; arrange over salad. Makes 4 servings.

Chinese Chicken Salad

The sweet-and-sour flavors of the marinade come through in this satisfying main-course salad.

1 lb	boneless skinless chicken breasts	500 g
1/4 cup	soy sauce	50 mL
1/4 cup	dry sherry	50 mL
1 tsp	ginger	5 mL
1	clove garlic, minced	1
1/4 lb	snow peas, trimmed	125 g
1/4 cup	chopped fresh coriander (optional)	50 mL
3 cups	shredded Chinese lettuce (napa)	750 mL
1 cup	bean sprouts	250 mL
4	green onions, thinly sliced	4
	DRESSING	
1/4 cup	sesame seeds	50 mL
1/4 cup	peanut oil	50 mL
2 tbsp	sesame oil	25 mL
2 tbsp	rice vinegar	25 mL
2 tsp	cornstarch	10 mL

■ Place chicken in heavy plastic bag set in dish. Mix together soy sauce, sherry, ginger and garlic. Pour over chicken; press air out of bag and secure closed. Marinate in refrigerator for at least 1 or up to 24 hours.

■ In pot of boiling water, cook snow peas for 30 seconds; drain immediately and cool under cold water. Drain and set aside. Trim and coarsely chop coriander (if using). In salad bowl, mix together lettuce, bean sprouts, onions, and coriander (if using).

■ **Dressing:** In large heavy skillet, toast sesame seeds over medium heat for 4 to 5 minutes or until golden, shaking pan frequently. Remove and set aside.

■ In same skillet, heat 1 tbsp (15 mL) of the peanut oil over medium-high heat until sizzling. Remove chicken from marinade, reserving 1/4 cup (50 mL). Cook chicken for about 4 minutes on each side or until no longer pink inside. Cut chicken into thin strips; add to salad bowl.

■ In small saucepan, combine reserved marinade, remaining peanut oil, sesame oil, vinegar and cornstarch; bring to boil and boil for 3 minutes, stirring constantly. Pour dressing over salad; toss gently. Sprinkle with sesame seeds; garnish with snow peas. Serve immediately. Makes about 4 servings.

Honey Apricot Chicken

The exotic flavors of Morocco dress up moist, tender chicken. Serve with rice or couscous.

1	**chicken (3-1/2 to 4 lb/1.75 to 2 kg)**	**1**
3/4 tsp	**each cumin, ginger and coriander**	**4 mL**
1/2 tsp	**turmeric**	**2 mL**
Pinch	**each cinnamon, salt and pepper**	**Pinch**
1 tbsp	**each butter and vegetable oil**	**15 mL**
2	**onions, thinly sliced**	**2**
2	**cloves garlic, minced**	**2**
1/2 cup	**chicken stock**	**125 mL**
1/3 cup	**liquid honey**	**75 mL**
2	**lemons, sliced**	**2**
	Cinnamon sticks (optional)	
1 tbsp	**cornstarch**	**15 mL**
4	**canned apricots, quartered**	**4**

■ Cut chicken into 8 pieces; remove skin. In large bowl, combine cumin, ginger, coriander, turmeric, cinnamon, salt and pepper. Add chicken; toss to coat.

■ In large skillet, melt butter with oil over medium-high heat; cook chicken for 10 to 12 minutes or until browned on all sides. Drain off all but 1 tbsp (15 mL) of the fat. Add onions and garlic; pour in 1/3 cup (75 mL) of the stock and honey, stirring and spooning over chicken.

■ Arrange half of the lemon slices over chicken; tuck in cinnamon sticks (if using). Bring to boil; reduce heat, cover and simmer, basting occasionally, for 25 to 30 minutes or until chicken is no longer pink inside.

■ Transfer chicken and cinnamon sticks to warm platter; keep warm. Discard lemon. Over high heat, bring liquid to boil. Blend remaining stock with cornstarch; whisk into skillet and cook, stirring constantly, for about 3 minutes or until smooth and thickened. Add remaining lemon and apricots; heat through. Taste and adjust seasoning. Pour over chicken. Makes 6 servings.

Chicken Paprika

Authentic Hungarian paprika is a delicate spice. "Sweet," with regard to paprika, means without strong spiciness, not sugary. It adds a gentle piquancy to this easy dish.

1	**chicken (about 5 lb/2.5 kg), cut in pieces**	**1**
2 tbsp	**vegetable oil**	**25 mL**
3 cups	**chopped onions**	**750 mL**
4 tsp	**Hungarian paprika**	**20 mL**
1 cup	**chopped peeled tomato (1 large)**	**250 mL**
1 cup	**chopped sweet green pepper (1 large)**	**250 mL**
1-1/2 tsp	**salt**	**7 mL**
1/4 cup	**sour cream**	**50 mL**

■ Wipe chicken and pat dry. In large skillet, heat oil over medium-low heat; cook onions, covered and stirring periodically, for 5 minutes without browning.

■ Add paprika and increase heat to medium-high; immediately nestle chicken pieces in onions. Cook, turning chicken occasionally, until golden-red all over.

■ Reduce heat to medium-low; stir in tomato, green pepper and salt. Cover and cook for about 30 minutes or until chicken is no longer pink inside and juices run clear when chicken is pierced.

■ Remove chicken to heated platter; skim off fat from pan juices. Pour mixture into food processor or food mill and purée. Stir in sour cream; taste and adjust seasoning. Spoon over chicken. Makes 6 servings.

Stir-Fried Chicken with Snow Peas and Cherry Tomatoes

This Chinese-style dish has a full fresh flavor and colorful appearance. Serve over steamed rice or noodles.

1-1/2 lb	**chicken breasts, skinned and boned**	**750 g**
1 tbsp	**cornstarch**	**15 mL**
1 tbsp	**rice wine**	**15 mL**
1 tbsp	**soy sauce**	**15 mL**
1	**egg white, lightly beaten**	**1**
1/3 cup	**peanut or corn oil**	**75 mL**
2	**cloves garlic, minced**	**2**
1 tbsp	**chopped gingerroot**	**15 mL**
2	**green onions, chopped**	**2**
3/4 lb	**snow peas**	**375 g**
2 cups	**cherry tomatoes**	**500 mL**
	Salt	

	SAUCE	
1/2 cup	**chicken stock**	**125 mL**
2 tbsp	**soy sauce**	**25 mL**
1 tbsp	**rice wine**	**15 mL**
2 tsp	**cornstarch**	**10 mL**
1 tsp	**sesame oil**	**5 mL**

■ Cut chicken into 1-1/2-inch (4 cm) cubes. In bowl, combine chicken, cornstarch, rice wine, soy sauce and egg white; let marinate at room temperature for 20 minutes.

■ **Sauce:** Combine chicken stock, soy sauce, rice wine, cornstarch and sesame oil; set aside.

■ In wok or skillet, heat 3 tbsp (50 mL) of the peanut oil over high heat; stir-fry chicken until no longer pink inside. Remove and set aside. Wipe out wok.

■ Add remaining oil to wok and heat; stir-fry garlic, gingerroot and onions for 1 minute or until fragrant. Add snow peas; stir-fry for 1 minute. Add tomatoes and reserved chicken; stir-fry for 1 minute.

■ Stir sauce and pour into wok; cook until boiling and thickened. Taste and adjust seasoning with salt if desired. Makes 4 to 6 servings.

Microwave Chicken and Sausage Paella

The microwave oven makes quick work of this robust rice, chicken and sausage casserole.

1/2 lb	**Italian sausages, cut in 1/2-inch (1 cm) slices**	**250 g**
1	**onion, chopped**	**1**
1	**sweet green pepper, chopped**	**1**
2	**cloves garlic, minced**	**2**
1 cup	**long-grain rice**	**250 mL**
1	**can (14 oz/398 mL) tomatoes (undrained), chopped**	**1**
1 cup	**chicken stock**	**250 mL**
1/2 tsp	**ground turmeric**	**2 mL**
Pinch	**cayenne pepper**	**Pinch**
1 lb	**boneless skinless chicken breasts, cut in 1-inch (2.5 cm) pieces**	**500 g**
	Salt and pepper	
1	**green onion, chopped**	**1**

■ In 12-cup (3 L) microwaveable casserole, combine sausages, onion, green pepper and garlic; microwave, uncovered, at High for 4 to 6 minutes or until vegetables are softened, stirring twice.

■ Stir in rice, tomatoes, chicken stock, turmeric and cayenne pepper; cover and microwave at High for 8 to 10 minutes or until boiling. Microwave at Medium (50%) for 5 minutes.

■ Stir in chicken; cover and microwave at Medium (50%) for 7 to 9 minutes or until rice is tender, chicken is no longer pink inside and most of the liquid has been absorbed. Let stand, covered, for 5 minutes. Season with salt and pepper to taste. Sprinkle with chopped green onion. Makes 4 to 6 servings.

Cumberland Chicken with Pork, Herb and Ham Stuffing

The aroma of the stuffing will set appetites at the ready for this delicious chicken dish.

12	**chicken thighs, boned**	**12**
	STUFFING	
1 tbsp	**butter**	**15 mL**
1/2 cup	**chopped onion**	**125 mL**
1/2 cup	**chopped mushrooms**	**125 mL**
1/2 cup	**chopped fresh spinach**	**125 mL**
2 tbsp	**chopped fresh parsley**	**25 mL**
1/4 tsp	**each dried marjoram, sage and thyme**	**1 mL**
1/4 tsp	**salt**	**1 mL**
	Pepper	
1/2 lb	**ground pork**	**250 g**
1/4 lb	**finely chopped ham**	**125 g**
3/4 cup	**soft bread crumbs**	**175 mL**
1	**egg**	**1**
	CUMBERLAND SAUCE	
1 cup	**red currant jelly**	**250 mL**
1/2 cup	**port**	**125 mL**
1/2 cup	**orange juice**	**125 mL**
1/4 cup	**lemon juice**	**50 mL**
	Rind of 1 orange, cut in slivers	
1/2 tsp	**dry mustard**	**2 mL**
1/2 tsp	**ginger**	**2 mL**

■ **Stuffing:** In skillet, melt butter over medium heat; cook onion until tender. Stir in mushrooms, spinach, parsley, marjoram, sage, thyme, salt, and pepper to taste; cook for 2 minutes or until fragrant. Let cool.

■ In bowl, combine pork, ham, bread crumbs and egg; add onion mixture and mix well. Fill pocket of each boned thigh with heaping tablespoon (15 mL) of stuffing and enclose with thigh meat. Secure with string. Place seam side down in single layer in greased baking dish.

■ **Cumberland Sauce:** In saucepan, combine jelly, port, orange juice, lemon juice, orange rind, mustard and ginger; bring to boil, stirring constantly. Remove from heat.

■ Pour 1/2 cup (125 mL) of the sauce over thighs. Bake, uncovered, in 350°F (180°C) oven for 1-1/4 hours, basting occasionally, or until golden brown and juices run clear when chicken is pierced. Remove string. Serve remaining sauce warm with chicken. Makes 8 to 12 servings.

Chicken Breasts with Herb Cheese Sauce

The herbs in cream cheese, such as Boursin or Rondelé, impart a wonderful flavor to this sauce. Serve with boiled potatoes and glazed carrots.

6	**chicken breasts, skinned and boned**	**6**
	Salt and pepper	
	All-purpose flour	
1/4 cup	**unsalted butter**	**50 mL**
6 oz	**herbed cream cheese, cubed**	**175 g**
1 cup	**whipping cream**	**250 mL**
2 tbsp	**chopped fresh parsley**	**25 mL**

■ Pat chicken dry; season with salt and pepper to taste. Dust lightly with flour.

■ In large heavy skillet, melt butter over medium heat; cook chicken for 5 to 6 minutes on each side or until no longer pink inside. Remove to serving platter and keep warm.

■ Pour off excess fat in skillet. Add cheese and cream; cook over medium heat, stirring constantly, until cheese melts and sauce thickens slightly. Taste and adjust seasoning. Pour over chicken; sprinkle with parsley. Makes 6 servings.

Lemon-Mustard Chicken Breasts

Serve this zippy lemon-mustard chicken with sweet red pepper strips and small parboiled potatoes that have been crisped and browned right on the barbecue. A light brush with oil will keep the vegetables moist.

4	**chicken breasts (about 1-1/2 lb/750 g total)**	**4**
2 tbsp	**minced green onion**	**25 mL**
2 tbsp	**Dijon mustard**	**25 mL**
1 tbsp	**vegetable oil**	**15 mL**
2 tsp	**coarsely grated lemon rind**	**10 mL**
1 tbsp	**lemon juice**	**15 mL**
1 tsp	**Worcestershire sauce**	**5 mL**
Pinch	**(approx) pepper**	**Pinch**
	Salt	

■ Set each breast bone side down. Starting at narrow end, cut meat away from bones using short strokes of knife angled toward bones. Remove skin if desired.

■ In nonaluminum bowl, stir together onion, Dijon mustard, oil, lemon rind and juice, Worcestershire sauce and pepper; add chicken and turn to coat. Cover and marinate in refrigerator for at least 2 or up to 8 hours.

■ Place breasts, skin side up, on greased grill over medium-hot coals or at medium-high setting. Grill for about 12 minutes, turning twice, or until golden brown and no longer pink inside. Season with salt and pepper to taste. Makes 4 servings.

Roast Young Chickens with Watercress

A simple but perfectly roasted chicken is a delight hot, or packed cold for a picnic.

2	**chickens (each 3 lb/1.5 kg)**	**2**
1/3 cup	**butter, softened**	**75 mL**
1 tsp	**grated lemon rind**	**5 mL**
1 tsp	**dry mustard**	**5 mL**
1/4 tsp	**pepper**	**1 mL**
2	**small onions**	**2**
2	**bay leaves**	**2**
2	**sprigs fresh thyme (or 1 tsp/5 mL dried)**	**2**
1 tsp	**dried marjoram**	**5 mL**
	Salt	
2	**bunches watercress**	**2**

■ Wipe chickens dry inside and out. Combine butter, lemon rind, mustard and pepper; set aside.

■ Into cavity of each chicken, place onion, bay leaf, thyme sprig and half of the marjoram. Skewer cavities closed; tie wings to bodies and legs together with string.

■ Spread butter mixture evenly over chickens. Place breast side up on rack in shallow roasting pan; roast in 325°F (160°C) oven, basting occasionally, for 1-1/2 hours or until golden and meat thermometer registers 185°F (85°C). Season with salt to taste. Let stand for 5 minutes. Remove coarse stems from watercress. Arrange watercress and chickens on large platter. Makes 12 servings.

Honey-Citrus Chicken Kabobs

Chicken and sweet pepper are threaded onto skewers, then broiled for a tasty meal.

1 lb	**boneless skinless chicken breasts**	**500 g**
1/4 cup	**liquid honey**	**50 mL**
1/4 cup	**orange juice**	**50 mL**
2 tbsp	**lemon juice**	**25 mL**
1/2 tsp	**each grated orange and lemon rind**	**2 mL**
1/2 tsp	**ginger**	**2 mL**
1	**large sweet red or green pepper**	**1**

■ Cut chicken into 1-inch (2.5 cm) pieces; place in plastic bag in bowl.

■ In microwaveable bowl or saucepan, combine honey, orange and lemon juices and rinds; stir in ginger and microwave at High for 30 seconds or heat on stove top until honey dissolves. Pour over chicken and mix to coat. Press air out of bag and seal; refrigerate for at least 2 hours or for up to 12 hours.

■ Cut red pepper into 1-inch (2.5 cm) pieces. Drain chicken and reserve marinade. Alternately thread chicken and red pepper onto 4 oiled skewers. Broil kabobs about 5 inches (12 cm) from heat, turning once and brushing with reserved marinade, for 8 minutes or until chicken is tender and no longer pink inside. Makes 4 servings.

Chicken Teriyaki

This Japanese-style chicken dish is sweet and delicious. If you wish to serve it in the authentic Japanese manner, cut each serving into about 8 pieces for easy grasping with chopsticks. This is also great on the barbecue. Serve with steamed rice and sautéed snow peas.

6	**chicken breasts**	**6**
1/4 cup	**granulated sugar**	**50 mL**
1/4 cup	**soy sauce**	**50 mL**
1/4 cup	**Japanese cooking wine or sherry**	**50 mL**
1	**clove garlic, minced**	**1**
1 tbsp	**coarsley chopped gingerroot**	**15 mL**
	Vegetable oil	

■ Pat chicken dry. In saucepan, combine sugar, soy sauce, cooking wine, garlic and gingerroot; cook over medium heat for 5 to 10 minutes or until slightly syrupy.

■ Brush broiler pan with oil; place 4 inches (10 cm) from heat until hot. Arrange chicken on pan; brush with some of the sauce. Broil for 5 minutes; brush with sauce and broil for 5 minutes longer. Turn chicken over and repeat, broiling until no longer pink inside. Makes 6 servings.

Chicken Breasts with Strawberries and Pink Peppercorns

A summery delight, this main course is wonderful either hot or cold. If pink peppercorns are unavailable, add a heavy coarse grinding of white or black peppercorns.

4	**boneless skinless chicken breasts**	**4**
	All-purpose flour	
2 tbsp	**butter**	**25 mL**
1 tbsp	**vegetable oil**	**15 mL**
1/4 cup	**chopped shallots**	**50 mL**
1/4 cup	**white wine or chicken stock**	**50 mL**
2 tbsp	**strawberry or white wine vinegar**	**25 mL**
2 tsp	**pink peppercorns**	**10 mL**
1 cup	**strawberries, halved**	**250 mL**

■ Dredge chicken breasts with flour. In large skillet, heat 1 tbsp (15 mL) of the butter with oil over medium-high heat; cook chicken, turning once, for about 6 minutes or until golden brown and no longer pink inside. Remove to serving platter and keep warm.

■ Pour off excess fat from skillet and melt remaining butter; cook shallots, stirring, for about 2 minutes or until tender.

■ Add wine, vinegar and pink peppercorns; bring to boil, stirring to scrape up browned bits from bottom of pan. Boil for about 2 minutes or until syrupy and reduced to about 2 tbsp (25 mL). Add strawberries; stir just to coat. Immediately pour over chicken and serve. Makes 4 servings.

Chicken, Almonds and Pearl Onions

If you'd like a slightly thicker sauce for this dish, stir 1 tsp (5 mL) cornstarch into the chicken stock before adding to skillet.

1 cup	**pearl onions**	**250 mL**
1 tbsp	**butter**	**15 mL**
1 tbsp	**vegetable oil**	**15 mL**
1	**strip lemon rind**	**1**
1/2 tsp	**packed brown sugar**	**2 mL**
3/4 lb	**chicken breasts**	**375 g**
1/4 cup	**blanched whole almonds**	**50 mL**
1/2 cup	**chicken stock**	**125 mL**
Pinch	**nutmeg**	**Pinch**
	Salt and pepper	

■ Cover pearl onions with boiling water; let stand for 2 minutes. Drain and slip off skins; make small slit in root ends.

■ In skillet, melt butter with oil over medium heat; add onions and lemon rind. Sprinkle with sugar; cover and cook for 3 minutes.

■ Meanwhile, slice chicken across the grain into 1-inch (2.5 cm) wide strips. Increase heat to high; remove and discard lemon rind. Add chicken and almonds; cook, stirring, for 2 minutes or until onions and almonds are golden.

■ Stir in stock, scraping up any browned bits in skillet. Add nutmeg, and salt and pepper to taste. Reduce heat to low; cook, covered, for 2 to 3 minutes or until onions are tender-crisp and chicken is no longer pink inside. Makes 4 servings.

CHICKEN CHECKLIST

Store chicken in the coldest part of the fridge for up to 48 hours, or in freezer for up to six months.

- *Rinse, pat dry and rewrap chicken if not using immediately or if freezing.*
- *Store on tray on lowest shelf of fridge to prevent juices from dripping onto other food.*
- *Serve cooked chicken on clean platter, never on one that's held raw chicken or other meats.*
- *Refrigerate leftover chicken immediately without waiting for it to cool.*
- *Wash hands with hot soapy water before and after handling raw poultry.*
- *Use a plastic (polyethylene) chopping board and immediately after using, wash board, utensils and knives in hot soapy water with a few drops of chlorine bleach. Rinse well and dry.*
- *Cook chicken until it reaches internal temperature of 185°F (85°C). White meat should show no trace of pink, and juices of dark meat should run clear when chicken is pierced with a fork.*
- *To cut calories and fat, remove the skin from chicken after cooking. An average-size breast, roasted, chalks up about 195 calories with skin, 140 without. And you'll be eating less than half the amount of fat: three grams compared with almost eight.*

Chicken with Lemon Sauce

For a simple accompaniment, serve this chicken dish with buttered noodles.

8	**boneless skinless chicken breasts (about 3 lb/1.5 kg total)**	**8**
1	**egg**	**1**
2 tbsp	**milk**	**25 mL**
1 cup	**ground almonds, toasted***	**250 mL**
1/2 cup	**dry bread crumbs**	**125 mL**
1/2 tsp	**white pepper**	**2 mL**
	All-purpose flour	
3 tbsp	**vegetable oil**	**50 mL**
2 tbsp	**butter**	**25 mL**

	LEMON SAUCE	
1 tbsp	**butter**	**15 mL**
4 tsp	**all-purpose flour**	**20 mL**
1 cup	**chicken stock**	**250 mL**
2	**egg yolks**	**2**
1 tbsp	**lemon juice**	**15 mL**
1 tsp	**grated lemon rind**	**5 mL**
	Salt and pepper	

■ Pat chicken dry. Beat egg with milk. Mix almonds with bread crumbs and pepper. Lightly dust chicken with flour; dip into egg mixture, letting excess drip off. Dip into almond mixture to coat completely. Place on rack and cover with tea towel; refrigerate for at least 1 or up to 6 hours.

■ On 15- × 10-inch (40 × 25 cm) jelly roll pan, heat oil and butter in 375°F (190°C) oven for 5 minutes. Place chicken breasts in single layer on pan; bake for 20 to 25 minutes or until no longer pink inside, turning halfway through. Remove to serving platter.

■ **Lemon Sauce:** In saucepan, melt butter over medium-high heat; whisk in flour, stirring for 30 seconds. Gradually whisk in stock; cook, stirring constantly, for 4 to 5 minutes or until boiling and thickened slightly. Reduce heat to low.

■ Whisk egg yolks with lemon juice; whisk into sauce and cook, stirring constantly, for 2 to 3 minutes or until sauce lightly coats wooden spoon (do not boil). Stir in lemon rind; season with salt and pepper to taste. Pour over chicken. Makes 8 servings.

*To toast almonds, heat in small skillet over low heat until lightly browned, about 5 minutes.

Chicken à la King

Aren't you glad old-fashioned comfort food is back? Make this with either chicken or turkey, and serve it in patty shells or on toast or split tea biscuits.

3 tbsp	butter	45 mL
3/4 cup	sliced mushrooms	175 mL
1/4 cup	chopped onion	50 mL
1/4 cup	chopped celery	50 mL
1/4 cup	chopped sweet green pepper	50 mL
2 tbsp	all-purpose flour	25 mL
1 cup	light cream	250 mL
1/2 cup	chicken stock	125 mL
1 tbsp	dry sherry (optional)	15 mL
	Salt and pepper	
2 cups	cubed cooked chicken	500 mL
2 tbsp	chopped pimiento	25 mL

■ In skillet, melt 1 tbsp (15 mL) of the butter over medium heat; cook mushrooms, onion, celery and green pepper just until tender. With slotted spoon, remove vegetable mixture and set aside.

■ To skillet, add remaining butter; heat until melted. Stir in flour; heat until bubbling. Stir in cream and stock; cook, stirring constantly, until boiling and thickened. Cook for about 2 minutes longer or until no raw taste of starch remains. Stir in sherry (if using); season with salt and pepper to taste.

■ Stir in reserved vegetable mixture, chicken and pimiento. Cook, stirring occasionally, until heated through. Makes 4 servings.

Roast Chicken with Lemon and Rosemary

Lemon and rosemary add subtle flavor to roast chicken. Avoid the powdered rosemary; crumble the crushed dried variety.

1	chicken (3-1/2 lb/1.75 kg)	1
1 tbsp	dried rosemary	15 mL
1	lemon, halved	1
1/4 cup	chicken stock	50 mL

■ Pat chicken dry inside and out; sprinkle with rosemary inside and out. Place one lemon half inside cavity; squeeze juice from other half over chicken. Truss chicken and place on greased rack in roasting pan.

■ Roast in 325°F (160°C) oven, tipping pan to let juices run from cavity and basting chicken occasionally, for 2 hours or until juices run clear and meat thermometer registers 185°F (85°C). Discard lemon.

■ Transfer chicken to platter; skim off fat from pan juices. Add stock to pan and stir over medium heat to scrape up brown bits; strain and serve with chicken. Makes 4 servings.

Coriander-Orange Chicken

Oranges and fragrant coriander add a good-enough-for-company taste to chicken breasts. To save money, buy skin-on, bone-in chicken breasts. Pull off skin; starting along the breastbone and using a sharp paring knife to cut close to the bones, ease breast meat off in one piece. Use bones to make chicken stock.

4	**boneless skinless chicken breasts**	**4**
1-1/2 tsp	**ground coriander**	**7 mL**
Pinch	**cinnamon**	**Pinch**
	Salt and pepper	
2 tbsp	**butter**	**25 mL**
1	**onion, chopped**	**1**
1	**clove garlic, minced**	**1**
1 tsp	**coarsely grated orange rind**	**5 mL**
1/2 cup	**orange juice**	**125 mL**
1/2 cup	**dry white vermouth or chicken stock**	**125 mL**
1	**orange**	**1**

■ If desired, place chicken breasts between plastic wrap and pound until flattened to about 1/4-inch (5 mm) thickness. Blend coriander, cinnamon, and salt and pepper to taste; rub into chicken.

■ In large skillet, melt butter over medium-high heat; brown chicken well on both sides, 4 to 6 minutes or until no longer pink inside. Remove and keep warm.

■ Reduce heat to low; cook onion and garlic, covered, for about 4 minutes or until softened. Add orange rind, juice and vermouth; bring to boil and boil hard for about 4 minutes or until syrupy.

■ Return chicken and any juices to pan, turning to coat well with sauce. Cook until heated through; season with salt and pepper to taste. Halve orange lengthwise; slice crosswise and fan around chicken. Makes 4 servings.

Scalloped Oysters and Chicken

Oysters add a festive flavor to this easy-to-make dish. Be sure to use fresh (not canned) oysters. For a sit-down dinner, you may substitute chicken pieces for the boneless breasts.

2 lb	**boneless chicken breasts**	**1 kg**
1 cup	**butter**	**250 mL**
1/2 cup	**dry white wine**	**125 mL**
3 cups	**fine cracker crumbs**	**750 mL**
3-1/2 cups	**fresh-shucked medium or small oysters (about 1-3/4 lb/ 875 g) with liquor reserved**	**875 mL**
3/4 cup	**whipping cream**	**175 mL**
2 tbsp	**aromatic bitters**	**25 mL**
2 tsp	**Worcestershire sauce**	**10 mL**
1-1/2 tsp	**salt**	**7 mL**
1/2 tsp	**pepper**	**2 mL**
1/2 tsp	**dried thyme**	**2 mL**
Dash	**hot pepper sauce (or pinch cayenne pepper)**	**Dash**
	Fresh parsley sprigs	

■ Cut chicken into bite-size pieces. In skillet, heat 1/4 cup (50 mL) of the butter over medium-high heat; brown chicken, in batches. Remove chicken and set aside.

■ Pour off fat in skillet; add wine and bring to boil, scraping up browned bits from pan. Remove from heat.

■ In saucepan, melt remaining butter; toss with crumbs. Set aside.

■ Drain oysters, reserving liquor in measure; add enough water if necessary to make 3/4 cup (175 mL).

■ Pat one-third of the crumbs into greased 13- × 9-inch (3 L) baking dish. Combine chicken with oysters; arrange half of the mixture over crumbs. Pat half of the remaining crumbs on top; cover with remaining oyster mixture. Pat remaining crumbs on top.

■ Combine oyster liquor, wine mixture, whipping cream, aromatic bitters, Worcestershire sauce, salt, pepper, thyme and hot pepper sauce; pour over casserole. Bake in 375°F (190°C) oven for 20 to 25 minutes or until bubbling and heated through. Garnish with parsley. Serve immediately. Makes 8 servings.

(centre) Scalloped Oysters and Chicken ►

Chicken Breasts with Curry Orange Sauce

Here's a quick and easy chicken dish that's special enough to serve to company.

1	**large orange**	**1**
4	**boneless skinless chicken breasts, pounded thin**	**4**
1/2 tsp	**salt**	**2 mL**
1/4 tsp	**pepper**	**1 mL**
2 tsp	**all-purpose flour**	**10 mL**
1/4 cup	**butter**	**50 mL**
2	**green onions, chopped**	**2**
1/2 cup	**chicken stock**	**125 mL**
1 tsp	**lime juice**	**5 mL**
Pinch	**curry powder**	**Pinch**

■ Grate rind from orange; set aside. Peel and section orange, discarding white pith; set aside.

■ Season chicken with salt and pepper; dust with flour. In large heavy skillet, heat 2 tbsp (25 mL) of the butter over medium-high heat; sauté chicken until lightly browned on both sides, about 3 minutes. Remove from pan and set aside.

■ Add 1 tbsp (15 mL) of the remaining butter to pan; cook onions until softened, about 1 minute. Add onions to chicken.

■ Drain any excess fat from pan; pour in stock. Bring to boil, stirring to scrape up any browned bits from bottom of pan. Stir in lime juice, curry powder and orange rind; cook for 1 minute. Return chicken and onions to pan. Reduce heat to low and simmer, covered, for 3 minutes or until chicken is no longer pink inside.

■ Using slotted spoon, transfer chicken to serving platter. Add remaining 1 tbsp (15 mL) butter to pan; cook, stirring, for 1 minute or until sauce has thickened slightly. Spoon over chicken. Garnish with orange sections. Makes 4 servings.

Creamy Chicken and Leeks with Pasta Shells

The strong anchovy taste disappears during cooking, lending a wonderful subtle flavor to this creamy chicken sauté.

4	**boneless skinless chicken breasts**	**4**
1/4 cup	**olive oil**	**50 mL**
2	**cloves garlic, minced**	**2**
4	**anchovy fillets, chopped (or 2 tsp/10 mL anchovy paste)**	**4**
4	**leeks (white parts only), sliced**	**4**
1 cup	**dry white wine**	**250 mL**
1/2 tsp	**dried rosemary**	**2 mL**
Pinch	**each black and cayenne peppers**	**Pinch**
1 cup	**whipping cream**	**250 mL**
2 cups	**shredded spinach**	**500 mL**
1/3 cup	**freshly grated Parmesan cheese**	**75 mL**
3/4 lb	**pasta shells or bow ties**	**375 g**
1 tbsp	**butter**	**15 mL**

■ Cut chicken into strips 2 inches (5 cm) long and 1/2 inch (1 cm) wide; set aside.

■ In large skillet, heat oil over medium heat; cook garlic, anchovies and leeks for 2 minutes or until garlic and leeks are softened. Add chicken and cook, stirring occasionally, for about 4 minutes or until chicken is no longer pink inside. With slotted spoon, remove chicken only and set aside.

■ Add wine, rosemary, and black and cayenne peppers to skillet; bring to boil and cook for 2 minutes. Stir in cream and return to boil; reduce heat to low and simmer for 1 minute or until thickened slightly. Return chicken to skillet; stir in spinach and Parmesan cheese and heat until sauce is bubbling.

■ Meanwhile, in large pot of boiling salted water, cook pasta until tender but firm. Drain well and toss with butter. Transfer to warmed serving bowl; pour chicken mixture over top. Makes 4 servings.

Orange and Apricot Roast Chicken

Glazed to a rich brown color, this simply roasted chicken offers the refreshing flavor combination of oranges and apricots.

1	**chicken (about 3 lb/1.5 kg)**	**1**
	Salt and pepper	
2	**oranges (unpeeled), sliced**	**2**
1 tbsp	**each butter and vegetable oil**	**15 mL**
1/2 cup	**orange juice**	**125 mL**
12	**dried apricots**	**12**
1/4 cup	**packed brown sugar**	**50 mL**
2 tbsp	**cider vinegar**	**25 mL**
1 tbsp	**grated orange rind**	**15 mL**
2 tsp	**Dijon mustard**	**10 mL**
1 tbsp	**cornstarch**	**15 mL**
3/4 cup	**cold water**	**175 mL**
	Parsley or watercress sprigs (optional)	

■ Pat chicken dry; sprinkle inside with salt and pepper. Place half of the orange slices inside; truss chicken.

■ In small roasting pan, melt butter with oil over medium-high heat; add chicken and cook for 4 to 5 minutes or until browned all over. Roast, breast side up, uncovered, in 375°F (190°C) oven for 45 minutes.

■ Meanwhile, in small saucepan, bring orange juice to boil. Remove from heat; add apricots. Let soak for 20 minutes. Remove apricots; set aside.

■ To saucepan, add sugar, vinegar, orange rind and mustard; bring to boil. Boil, uncovered, for 3 to 5 minutes or until slightly thickened.

■ Pour half of the juice mixture over chicken; arrange apricots around chicken. Roast for 10 minutes longer. Brush with remaining juice mixture; roast for 10 to 15 minutes or until thermometer registers 185°F (85°C). Remove chicken and apricots to hot platter; cover loosely with foil. Remove fat from pan drippings.

■ Blend cornstarch with water; stir into pan drippings. Cook over medium-high heat for 2 minutes, stirring constantly, until smooth and thickened. Season with salt and pepper to taste.

■ Garnish chicken with remaining orange slices, and parsley (if using). Makes about 4 servings.

Chicken Breasts Normandy Style

Chicken, apples and cream are specialties of the north of France. The area is famous for its Calvados, an apple brandy. Here's a recipe that adapts particularly well to Canadian ingredients. Serve with rice pilaf and steamed broccoli.

6	**chicken breasts, skinned and boned**	**6**
	Salt and pepper	
	All-purpose flour	
3 tbsp	**unsalted butter**	**50 mL**
1	**onion, finely chopped**	**1**
2	**stalks celery, finely chopped**	**2**
2	**apples, peeled, cored and chopped**	**2**
2 tbsp	**brandy or Calvados**	**25 mL**
1/2 cup	**apple cider, white wine or chicken stock**	**125 mL**
3/4 cup	**whipping cream**	**175 mL**
2	**egg yolks**	**2**
2 tbsp	**toasted sliced almonds**	**25 mL**

■ Pat chicken dry; season with salt and pepper to taste. Dust lightly with flour.

■ In large skillet, melt butter over medium-high heat; brown chicken lightly on both sides. Remove from pan.

■ Pour off all but 2 tbsp (25 mL) fat in pan. Add onion, celery and apples; cook until vegetables and apples are tender and fragrant.

■ Add brandy and apple cider; bring to boil. Return chicken to pan and reduce heat; cover with greased waxed paper and cook gently for about 15 minutes or until no longer pink inside. Transfer chicken to serving platter and keep warm.

■ Transfer vegetable mixture to blender or food processor; purée and return to pan. Bring to boil and cook until reduced to about 1 cup (250 mL). Add 1/2 cup (125 mL) of the cream; bring to boil and cook until reduced slightly. Remove from heat.

■ Mix together egg yolks and remaining cream; stir in a little of the hot sauce. Stir yolk mixture back into pan. Cook over low heat, stirring, until sauce is slightly thickened. Taste and adjust seasoning. Pour over chicken; sprinkle with almonds. Makes 6 servings.

Jamaican Jerked Chicken

Allspice gives this Caribbean barbecued chicken its unique flavor and hot pepper its heat.

1/2 cup	**minced green onions**	**125 mL**
1/4 cup	**orange juice**	**50 mL**
1 tbsp	**minced gingerroot**	**15 mL**
1 tbsp	**minced hot pepper**	**15 mL**
1 tbsp	**lime or lemon juice**	**15 mL**
1 tbsp	**light soy sauce**	**15 mL**
1	**clove garlic, minced**	**1**
1 tsp	**allspice**	**5 mL**
1/4 tsp	**cinnamon**	**1 mL**
Pinch	**cloves**	**Pinch**
2 lb	**chicken thighs**	**1 kg**

■ In shallow glass dish, combine onions, orange juice, gingerroot, hot pepper, lime juice, soy sauce, garlic, allspice, cinnamon and cloves. Add chicken; cover and marinate in refrigerator, turning occasionally, for at least 2 or up to 8 hours.

■ Remove chicken from marinade; brush any hot pepper off chicken back into marinade and reserve.

■ Place chicken on greased grill over medium-hot coals or at medium setting; cook, turning occasionally, for 15 minutes. Drizzle with marinade; cook, drizzling with remaining marinade, for 15 to 25 minutes longer or until juices run clear when chicken is pierced. Makes 4 servings.

BARBECUING CHICKEN PARTS
Place chicken directly on the grill; brush with vegetable oil or marinade and turn frequently to prevent burning. Barbecue for 7 to 8 minutes per side for wings, 6 to 7 minutes per side for boneless breasts, 30 to 40 minutes for pieces and 50 to 55 minutes for chicken halves.

Chicken with Tomatoes and Corn

Fresh juicy tomatoes and tender sweet corn complement each other in this saucy baked chicken dish. Bake corn bread (see Quick Corn Bread, p. 50) in special corn-on-the-cob-shaped loaf pans for a fun accompaniment.

6	**large chicken drumsticks**	**6**
1/4 cup	**all-purpose flour**	**50 mL**
2 tsp	**paprika**	**10 mL**
1/2 tsp	**each salt and pepper**	**2 mL**
2 tbsp	**butter**	**25 mL**
2 tbsp	**vegetable oil**	**25 mL**
1/2 cup	**chopped onion**	**125 mL**
1 cup	**tomato juice**	**250 mL**
1 tbsp	**chopped fresh basil**	**15 mL**
3	**tomatoes, peeled, quartered and seeded**	**3**
2	**cobs corn, husked and cut in chunks**	**2**
	Fresh basil leaves	

■ Rinse chicken; pat dry. In bag, combine flour, paprika, salt and pepper; add drumsticks, a few at a time, and shake to coat evenly. Reserve 1 tbsp (15 mL) of the flour mixture.

■ In large ovenproof skillet, heat butter with oil over medium heat; cook chicken for about 5 minutes on each side or until browned. Remove and keep warm.

■ Add onion to skillet; cook until tender, 2 to 3 minutes. Blend in reserved flour mixture. Stir in tomato juice and chopped basil. Finely dice 1 of the tomatoes; add to skillet and bring to boil. Reduce heat and simmer, stirring often, until thickened, 5 to 8 minutes. Taste and adjust seasoning if necessary.

■ Return chicken to skillet; add corn. Cover and bake in 350°F (180°C) oven for 15 minutes. Turn corn; add remaining tomatoes. Bake for 10 to 15 minutes longer or until juices run clear when chicken is pierced, basting once or twice. Makes 4 to 6 servings.

Ginger-Lime Chicken with Salsa

Serve remaining salsa over baked potatoes for an interesting side dish the next day.

1 tbsp	**vegetable oil**	**15 mL**
1/4 tsp	**grated lime rind**	**1 mL**
2 tsp	**lime juice**	**10 mL**
1 tsp	**Dijon mustard**	**5 mL**
1 tsp	**grated gingerroot**	**5 mL**
4	**boneless skinless chicken breasts**	**4**
	Pepper	
	Salsa (recipe follows)	

■ In bowl, whisk together oil, lime rind and juice, mustard and gingerroot; add chicken, turning to coat. Marinate, covered, in refrigerator for at least 1 hour or up to 8 hours.

■ On greased grill over medium-hot coals or on medium-high setting, cook chicken for 4 to 6 minutes per side or until no longer pink inside. Sprinkle with pepper to taste. Serve with Salsa. Makes 4 servings.

	SALSA	
1	**sweet red pepper**	**1**
1-1/2 tsp	**vegetable oil**	**7 mL**
1	**clove garlic, minced**	**1**
1-1/2 cups	**diced seeded peeled tomatoes**	**375 mL**
1 tbsp	**chopped fresh coriander or parsley**	**15 mL**
1 tbsp	**chopped fresh mint**	**15 mL**
1 tbsp	**white wine vinegar**	**15 mL**
1 tsp	**lime juice**	**5 mL**
1/2 tsp	**granulated sugar**	**2 mL**
Pinch	**salt**	**Pinch**
	Hot pepper sauce	

■ Broil or grill pepper until charred on all sides, about 15 minutes. Let cool; peel, seed and chop. Set aside in bowl.

■ In skillet, heat oil over medium heat; cook garlic for 3 to 5 minutes or until softened but not browned. Add to red pepper along with tomatoes, coriander, mint, vinegar, lime juice, sugar, salt, and dash hot pepper sauce or to taste. *(Salsa can be covered and refrigerated for up to 1 day.)* Makes about 2 cups (500 mL).

Spinach-Stuffed Chicken Legs

This recipe lets you take delicious advantage of the frequent supermarket specials on chicken quarters. You can substitute thawed, drained, chopped spinach for the cooked.

4	**chicken legs**	**4**
1 tbsp	**butter**	**15 mL**
4	**small mushrooms, chopped**	**4**
1	**green onion, chopped**	**1**
1	**clove garlic, minced**	**1**
1	**pkg (10 oz/284 g) spinach, trimmed**	**1**
1	**egg, beaten**	**1**
1/4 cup	**freshly grated Parmesan cheese**	**50 mL**
1/4 cup	**crushed soda crackers**	**50 mL**
	Pepper and paprika	

■ With fingers, carefully loosen but don't separate chicken skin from meat; set aside.

■ In skillet, melt butter over medium heat; cook mushrooms, onion and garlic for 3 minutes or until juices evaporate. Transfer to bowl.

■ Rinse spinach under cold water; add to pan with just the water clinging to leaves. Cook for 1 minute or just until wilted. Remove and let cool slightly. Squeeze out moisture to make about 1/2 cup (125 mL) spinach; chop and add to mushroom mixture. Blend in egg, cheese and cracker crumbs.

■ Stuff about 1/4 cup (50 mL) spinach mixture under skin of each leg. Arrange in greased baking pan; sprinkle with pepper and paprika to taste. Bake, uncovered and basting occasionally, in 350°F (180°C) oven for 45 minutes or until juices run clear when chicken is pierced. Makes 4 servings.

Chicken Cacciatore with Artichokes

Artichoke hearts and herbs lend this dish its savory appeal. The casserole freezes well, perfect to have on hand for unexpected company.

1	**jar (6 oz/170 mL) marinated artichoke hearts**	**1**
2 tbsp	**olive oil**	**25 mL**
3 lb	**chicken pieces**	**1.5 kg**
3 tbsp	**all-purpose flour**	**50 mL**
1	**can (28 oz/796 mL) plum tomatoes (undrained), chopped**	**1**
1/2 cup	**dry white wine or sherry**	**125 mL**
2	**cloves garlic, minced**	**2**
1/2 lb	**mushrooms, sliced**	**250 g**
1 tsp	**each chopped fresh oregano and basil (or 1/2 tsp/2 mL each dried)**	**5 mL**
1/2 tsp	**pepper**	**2 mL**
	Chopped fresh parsley	

■ Drain marinade from artichokes into large skillet; add oil and heat over medium-high heat. Dredge chicken in flour; cook, turning often, for 15 to 20 minutes or until well browned all over. Transfer to 12-cup (3 L) baking dish.

■ Discard all but 2 tbsp (25 mL) fat from skillet. Add tomatoes and juices, artichokes, wine, garlic, mushrooms, oregano, basil and pepper, stirring to scrape up any browned bits on bottom of pan. Pour over chicken. Bake, loosely covered, in 350°F (180°C) oven for 40 to 45 minutes or until chicken is no longer pink inside and juices run clear when chicken is pierced. Garnish with parsley. Makes 4 to 6 servings.

Greek-Style Chicken Casserole

This zesty chicken casserole is a meal in itself when served with a crisp salad and bread. If feta cheese is unavailable, use mozzarella.

4	**chicken legs (about 1-1/2 lb/750 g)**	**4**
2 tbsp	**olive oil**	**25 mL**
2	**cloves garlic, minced**	**2**
1	**onion, chopped**	**1**
1	**can (19 oz/540 mL) tomatoes (undrained)**	**1**
1	**can (7-1/2 oz/213 mL) tomato sauce**	**1**
1/4 cup	**dry white wine or chicken stock**	**50 mL**
1/4 tsp	**each salt, granulated sugar and dried oregano**	**1 mL**
Pinch	**pepper**	**Pinch**
1 cup	**macaroni (about 4 oz/125 g)**	**250 mL**
12	**black olives (preferably oil-cured)**	**12**
1/2 lb	**feta cheese, rinsed and crumbled**	**250 g**
2 tbsp	**chopped fresh parsley**	**25 mL**

■ Separate chicken legs at joints; wipe dry. In Dutch oven, heat oil over medium-high heat; sauté chicken until browned all over, 8 to 10 minutes. Set aside.

■ Pour off all but 2 tbsp (25 mL) of the fat. Add garlic and onion; cook for about 3 minutes or until softened. Stir in tomatoes, breaking up with wooden spoon. Add tomato sauce, wine, salt, sugar, oregano and pepper; bring to boil. Reduce heat and simmer, uncovered, for 5 to 10 minutes or until thickened. Return chicken to pan; cover and cook over medium-low heat for 15 to 20 minutes or until juices run clear when chicken is pierced.

■ Meanwhile, in large pot of boiling salted water, cook macaroni for about 8 minutes or until tender but firm; drain. Stir macaroni and olives into chicken mixture. Sprinkle with feta and parsley; bake in 425°F (220°C) oven for 10 to 15 minutes or until feta has melted. Makes about 4 servings.

Chicken Breasts with Hazelnut Cream Sauce

Hazelnuts add a wonderful flavor to many main-course dishes, including chicken. Serve this over fettuccine noodles.

4	**chicken breasts, skinned and boned**	**4**
	Salt and pepper	
	All-purpose flour	
3 tbsp	**unsalted butter**	**50 mL**
1 cup	**whipping cream**	**250 mL**
2 tbsp	**brandy or cognac**	**25 mL**
3/4 cup	**chopped toasted hazelnuts**	**175 mL**
1 lb	**fettuccine noodles**	**500 g**
Pinch	**nutmeg**	**Pinch**

■ Cut chicken into 2- × 1-inch (5 × 2.5 cm) strips. Season with salt and pepper to taste; dust lightly with flour.

■ In large heavy skillet, melt butter over medium-high heat; sauté chicken until lightly browned. Remove from pan.

■ Add cream and brandy to pan; bring to boil, stirring to scrape up browned bits from bottom of pan. Stir in nuts; cook for about 5 minutes or until sauce thickens slightly. Return chicken to pan; simmer gently, uncovered, for 5 minutes or until no longer pink inside.

■ Meanwhile, in large pot of boiling salted water, cook noodles until tender but firm. Drain well and place in pasta bowl or on platter. Toss with nutmeg; spoon sauce over top. Makes 4 to 6 servings.

SAUTÉING CHICKEN

Sautéing is one of the easiest and quickest ways to prepare chicken pieces. With a few extra ingredients — vegetables, such as onions, mushrooms or red peppers, and a simple sauce made with wine or cream and seasonings — you can add pizazz to ordinary chicken. Here's how:

- *Pat chicken dry with paper towels. Cook in hot fat over medium-high heat for 3 to 5 minutes per side, depending on thickness, or until browned on both sides; if using boneless chicken, remove and keep warm.*
- *Add any vegetables you are using to flavor the sauce, such as onions and mushrooms; cook until vegetables are tender and bone-in chicken is no longer pink. Remove chicken and keep warm.*
- *Drain off most of the fat from skillet. Deglaze pan by stirring in small amount of water, wine, chicken stock or whipping cream; cook over high heat, stirring and scraping up any flavorful brown bits from bottom of pan.*
- *Season with herbs, such as thyme, tarragon or basil, and salt and pepper to taste. If not serving immediately, return chicken to sauce and keep warm over low heat.*

Chicken Tetrazzini

Combine two favorites — chicken and spaghetti — in this make-ahead casserole.

3/4 lb	**spaghetti**	**375 g**
2 tbsp	**butter**	**25 mL**
3/4 cup	**sliced mushrooms**	**175 mL**
1	**stalk celery, chopped**	**1**
2	**green onions, chopped**	**2**
1/4 cup	**chopped sweet green pepper**	**50 mL**
3 tbsp	**all-purpose flour**	**50 mL**
1-1/2 cups	**chicken stock**	**375 mL**
1-1/2 cups	**low-fat milk**	**375 mL**
1/2 cup	**shredded Swiss or Cheddar cheese**	**125 mL**
1/2 tsp	**salt**	**2 mL**
1/4 tsp	**each pepper and dried marjoram**	**1 mL**
Pinch	**nutmeg**	**Pinch**
1-1/2 cups	**chopped cooked chicken**	**375 mL**

■ In saucepan of boiling salted water, cook spaghetti until tender but firm. Drain and rinse under cold water; set aside.

■ In large skillet, melt butter over medium heat; cook mushrooms, celery, onions and green pepper, stirring, for 3 minutes. Sprinkle with flour; cook, stirring, for 2 minutes.

■ Gradually pour in stock and milk; cook, stirring, for 5 to 7 minutes or until thickened. Stir in half of the cheese until melted. Add salt, pepper, marjoram and nutmeg; stir in chicken.

■ Combine spaghetti with sauce; taste and adjust seasonings. Place in greased 8-cup (2 L) casserole; sprinkle with remaining cheese. Bake in 350°F (180°C) oven for 20 to 25 minutes or until bubbling. Makes 4 servings.

Spicy Glazed Chicken Breasts with Corn Bread Dressing

This different and intriguing dish makes everyday chicken special. Make the corn bread yourself from this easy recipe or buy 8 medium-size cornmeal muffins.

8	**chicken breasts**	**8**
	DRESSING	
3 tbsp	**butter or vegetable oil**	**50 mL**
1	**onion, chopped**	**1**
2	**cloves garlic, finely chopped**	**2**
1	**stalk celery, chopped**	**1**
2	**sweet green peppers, diced**	**2**
1	**can (4 oz/113 mL) diced green chilies**	**1**
1/2 tsp	**salt**	**2 mL**
1/2 tsp	**pepper**	**2 mL**
4 cups	**diced Quick Corn Bread (recipe follows)**	**1 L**
2	**eggs, lightly beaten**	**2**
1 cup	**sour cream**	**250 mL**
1 cup	**shredded old Cheddar cheese**	**250 mL**
	GLAZE	
1/3 cup	**packed brown sugar**	**75 mL**
1/3 cup	**orange marmalade**	**75 mL**
2 tbsp	**lemon juice**	**25 mL**
1 tbsp	**Dijon mustard**	**15 mL**
2 tsp	**chili powder**	**10 mL**
1/2 tsp	**cayenne pepper**	**2 mL**
1/2 tsp	**paprika**	**2 mL**

■ **Dressing:** In large skillet, melt butter over medium heat; cook onion and garlic for 5 minutes or until tender and fragrant, stirring frequently. Add celery, green peppers, chilies, salt and pepper; cook for 10 minutes or until softened. Stir in corn bread.

■ Combine eggs, sour cream and cheese; stir into bread mixture until well moistened. Spoon into greased 12-cup (3 L) casserole dish. Bake in 350°F (180°C) oven for 30 to 40 minutes.

■ **Glaze:** Combine sugar, marmalade, lemon juice, mustard, chili powder, cayenne and paprika.

■ Pat chicken breasts dry. Arrange skin side up on foil-lined baking sheet; brush with some of the glaze. Bake in 350°F (180°C) oven, basting with glaze every 15 minutes, for 40 to 45 minutes or until chicken is no longer pink inside. Serve with dressing. Makes 6 to 8 servings.

	QUICK CORN BREAD	
1 cup	**all-purpose flour**	**250 mL**
1 cup	**cornmeal**	**250 mL**
2 tbsp	**granulated sugar**	**25 mL**
1 tbsp	**baking powder**	**15 mL**
1/2 tsp	**salt**	**2 mL**
2	**eggs**	**2**
1 cup	**milk**	**250 mL**
1/4 cup	**butter, melted**	**50 mL**

■ In bowl, combine flour, cornmeal, sugar, baking powder and salt. Combine eggs, milk and butter; stir into dry ingredients just until blended. Pour into greased 8-inch (2 L) square baking dish; bake in 375°F (190°C) oven for 30 to 35 minutes or until top is firm and tester comes out clean. Let cool on rack.

Chicken and Corn Sauté

For a southwestern flavor, serve this with light sour cream and corn chips.

2 tbsp	**vegetable oil**	**25 mL**
1	**onion, thinly sliced**	**1**
1	**clove garlic, minced**	**1**
Half	**sweet red or green pepper, thinly sliced**	**Half**
2	**boneless skinless chicken breasts, cut in 1/2-inch (1 cm) strips**	**2**
3/4 cup	**thawed or canned corn**	**175 mL**
3 tbsp	**ketchup or chili sauce**	**50 mL**
1/2 tsp	**chili powder**	**2 mL**
Pinch	**each salt and pepper**	**Pinch**
2 tbsp	**chopped fresh coriander or parsley**	**25 mL**

■ In large heavy nonstick skillet, heat oil over high heat; cook onion, garlic and red pepper for about 2 minutes or until tender. Using slotted spoon, transfer to dish and set aside.

■ Add chicken to skillet; cook for 2 to 4 minutes or until lightly browned and no longer pink inside. Add corn, ketchup, 1 tbsp (15 mL) water and chili powder; cook until heated through. Stir in onion mixture, salt and pepper. Spoon into serving dish; sprinkle with coriander. Makes 4 servings.

Chicken Sauté Niçoise

This dish is a cross between pan-fried chicken and stew. It takes only about 30 minutes to cook. Serve over rice or with boiled potatoes.

1	**chicken (about 3 lb/1.5 kg)**	**1**
	Salt and pepper	
	All-purpose flour	
3 tbsp	**vegetable oil**	**50 mL**
2	**onions, finely chopped**	**2**
2	**cloves garlic, finely chopped**	**2**
1 cup	**dry white wine**	**250 mL**
1 tbsp	**tomato paste**	**15 mL**
1 tsp	**each dried tarragon and thyme**	**5 mL**
1	**bay leaf**	**1**
1 cup	**black olives**	**250 mL**
2 tbsp	**capers**	**25 mL**
3 tbsp	**chopped fresh parsley**	**50 mL**

■ Cut chicken into about 12 pieces; pat dry. Season lightly with salt and pepper to taste; dust lightly with flour.

■ In large deep skillet, heat oil over medium-high heat; brown chicken pieces on all sides. Remove to plate.

■ Pour off all but 2 tbsp (25 mL) fat from pan. Add onions and garlic; cook until tender and fragrant but not browned. Add wine, tomato paste, tarragon, thyme, bay leaf, and salt and pepper to taste. Return chicken to pan; bring to boil. Reduce heat, cover and simmer gently for 30 minutes or until juices run clear when chicken is pierced and chicken is no longer pink inside.

■ Transfer chicken to serving platter and keep warm. Remove bay leaf. Add olives and capers to pan; cook over high heat, stirring constantly, until heated through and sauce is reduced to 3/4 cup (175 mL). Pour over chicken; sprinkle with parsley. Makes about 4 servings.

Chicken with Pasta and Peppers

Sweet peppers add a new twist to a deliciously easy chicken dish.

1 tbsp	olive oil	15 mL
2 lb	chicken parts	1 kg
2	onions, chopped	2
2	cloves garlic, minced	2
1 tsp	dried basil	5 mL
1/2 tsp	each dried oregano and thyme	2 mL
1	can (19 oz/540 mL) tomatoes (undrained)	1
1	can (14 oz/398 mL) tomato sauce	1
2 cups	coarsely chopped sweet peppers	500 mL
	Salt and pepper	
3/4 lb	corkscrew pasta or spaghetti	375 g
	Fresh basil leaves	

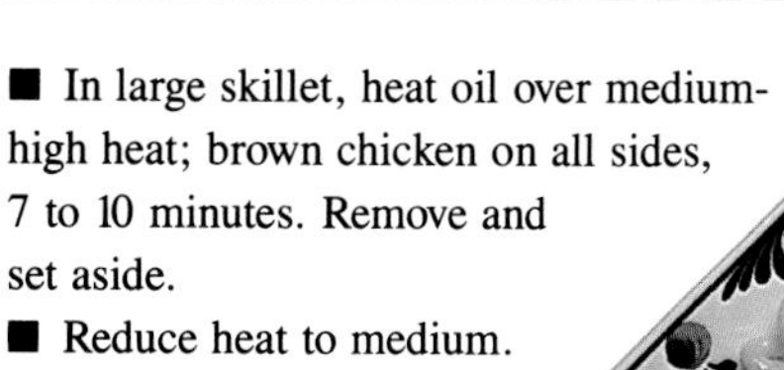

■ In large skillet, heat oil over medium-high heat; brown chicken on all sides, 7 to 10 minutes. Remove and set aside.

■ Reduce heat to medium. Add onions, garlic, basil, oregano and thyme; cook, stirring for 3 minutes. Add tomatoes, breaking up with fork; add tomato sauce.

■ Return chicken to skillet; bring sauce to boil. Reduce heat and simmer, turning chicken and stirring occasionally, for 30 minutes. Add peppers; cook for 5 to 10 minutes or until juices run clear when chicken is pierced. Season with salt and pepper to taste.

■ Meanwhile, in large pot of boiling salted water, cook pasta until tender but firm; drain and arrange on serving plate. Top with chicken mixture; garnish with fresh basil. Makes 4 to 6 servings.

Chicken Paella

For a special occasion, garnish this dish with shrimp and mussels.

1-1/2 tsp	vegetable oil	7 mL
1	onion, chopped	1
2	cloves garlic, minced	2
1 lb	boneless skinless chicken breasts, cut in 1-inch (2.5 cm) chunks	500 g
1	each sweet red and green pepper, cut in 1-inch (2.5 cm) chunks	1
1 cup	short-grain rice	250 mL
1	can (14 oz/398 mL) tomatoes, puréed	1
1/2 tsp	salt	2 mL
Pinch	pepper	Pinch
3/4 cup	chicken stock	175 mL
Pinch	saffron	Pinch
3 tbsp	chopped fresh parsley	50 mL

■ Brush deep skillet or Dutch oven with oil. Cook onion and garlic over medium heat for 3 to 5 minutes or until tender, adding 2 tbsp (25 mL) water if onion sticks to pan.

■ Add chicken and cook for 3 minutes, turning occasionally. Add red and green peppers and rice, stirring to coat well. Stir in tomatoes, salt and pepper.

■ Heat stock and stir in saffron until dissolved; add to pan and stir well. Bring to boil; reduce heat to low, cover and cook gently for 25 to 30 minutes or until most of the liquid has been absorbed and rice is tender. Taste and adjust seasoning. Sprinkle with parsley. Makes 4 servings.

Chicken with Artichokes and Lemons

Savor the fragrance of lemons and oregano in this slow-simmering chicken dish.

1	**chicken (about 3 lb/1.5 kg)**	**1**
2 tbsp	**olive oil**	**25 mL**
3	**onions, chopped**	**3**
2	**cloves garlic, minced**	**2**
1/4 cup	**dry sherry**	**50 mL**
1-1/2 cups	**chicken stock**	**375 mL**
2	**bay leaves**	**2**
1-1/2 tsp	**dried oregano**	**7 mL**
1-1/2 tsp	**dried mint**	**7 mL**
1/4 tsp	**pepper**	**1 mL**
1	**lemon**	**1**
16	**black olives**	**16**
2	**jars (each 6 oz/170 mL) marinated artichoke hearts, drained**	**2**
2 tbsp	**chopped fresh parsley**	**25 mL**

■ Cut chicken into 8 serving pieces. In large heavy skillet, heat oil over medium-high heat; brown chicken, in batches. Transfer to plate.

■ Pour off all but 1 tbsp (15 mL) fat from skillet; cook onions and garlic until softened, 3 to 4 minutes. Pour in sherry, stirring to scrape up brown bits from pan. Add stock, bay leaves, oregano, mint and pepper. Arrange chicken in pan in single layer.

■ Using sharp knife, peel lemon, removing white pith. Slice lemon and add to pan along with olives; bring to boil. Reduce heat, cover and simmer for 30 minutes.

■ Nestle artichoke hearts among chicken pieces; simmer for about 10 minutes longer or until chicken is no longer pink inside and juices run clear when chicken is pierced with fork. Discard bay leaves.

■ Using slotted spoon, transfer chicken, lemon, artichokes and olives to warm platter. Boil liquid over high heat for 3 to 5 minutes or until thickened slightly. Pour over chicken; garnish with parsley. Makes 4 to 6 servings.

Creamy Chicken with Vegetables

Serve this over whole wheat toast or in toasted hollowed-out grainy rolls. Fines herbes *— a mixture of parsley, chives, tarragon and sometimes chervil — add delicate flavor.*

1 tbsp	**vegetable oil**	**15 mL**
2 cups	**sliced mushrooms**	**500 mL**
1	**onion, chopped**	**1**
1/3 cup	**all-purpose flour**	**75 mL**
2-3/4 cups	**chicken stock**	**675 mL**
2	**carrots, diced**	**2**
1	**stalk celery, diced**	**1**
1-1/2 tsp	***fines herbes* or dried basil**	**7 mL**
1	**sweet red pepper, diced**	**1**
2-1/2 cups	**diced cooked chicken**	**625 mL**
1 cup	**frozen peas**	**250 mL**
1/4 cup	**plain yogurt**	**50 mL**
2 tbsp	**chopped fresh parsley**	**25 mL**
	Salt and pepper	

■ In large saucepan, heat oil over medium heat; cook mushrooms and onion for 3 minutes or until softened. Blend flour into stock and add to mushroom mixture; bring to boil over high heat and cook, stirring, for 3 to 5 minutes or until thickened and smooth.

■ Stir in carrots, celery and *fines herbes*; reduce heat to low, cover and simmer, stirring occasionally, for about 15 minutes or until vegetables are tender.

■ Add red pepper, chicken and peas; heat through. Remove from heat; stir in yogurt and parsley. Season with salt and pepper to taste. Makes 6 servings.

BUYING CHICKEN

Check skin for blemishes or discoloration. Normal skin can be white or yellow, depending on the chicken's feed and the depluming process. Yellow-skinned chickens often produce crisper skin.

- *When unwrapped, fresh chickens can have a chickeny odor that quickly dissipates, but they should have no lingering off-odors, and the package trays should be relatively free of liquid (the drier the package, the fresher the chicken). Always check the date on the package.*
- *Free-range chickens, available at markets and butcher shops, have been raised outside cages and are generally firmer and have a richer chicken flavor, but may not be quite as tender as supermarket poultry.*
- *The type of chicken you buy — whole, boneless, bone-in parts — depends on your budget, time and the recipe. Although separate chicken parts, especially boneless breasts and thighs, are more expensive than whole chickens, boneless chicken is very convenient when time is short.*

Chicken Breasts with Vermouth

This delectable dish takes only minutes to make. Prepare it for elegant occasions or as everyday fare.

4	**chicken breasts, skinned and boned**	**4**
	Salt and pepper	
	All-purpose flour	
1/4 cup	**unsalted butter**	**50 mL**
1	**shallot, finely chopped**	**1**
1/2 lb	**mushrooms, thinly sliced**	**250 g**
1/3 cup	**dry white vermouth**	**75 mL**
1 cup	**whipping cream**	**250 mL**

■ Slice chicken breasts in half horizontally to make 8 thin pieces; pat dry. Sprinkle with salt and pepper to taste; dust lightly with flour.

■ In large heavy skillet, melt half of the butter over medium heat; cook half of the chicken, turning occasionally, until no longer pink inside. Repeat with remaining butter and chicken. Remove to serving platter and keep warm.

■ Pour off excess fat in skillet; add shallot, mushrooms and vermouth. Bring to boil, stirring to scrape up browned bits from bottom of pan; cook until reduced to about 1/4 cup (50 mL).

■ Add cream and return to boil, stirring constantly; cook until thickened slightly. Taste and adjust seasoning. Pour over chicken and serve immediately. Makes about 4 servings.

Caribbean Chicken with Rice and Peas

Rice and Peas is a popular dish throughout the Caribbean. Sometimes coconut milk is used and adds a delicate sweet flavor. It is available canned in specialty food stores, Asian and West Indian shops.

1	chicken (about 2-1/2 lb/1.25 kg), cut in pieces	1
	Salt and pepper	
1/2 tsp	dried thyme	2 mL
1/4 cup	vegetable oil	50 mL
1	onion, chopped	1
2	cloves garlic, minced	2
1	small slice gingerroot, minced (optional)	1
1 tbsp	(approx) curry powder (preferably West Indian)	15 mL
1/2 cup	chicken stock	125 mL
	Hot pepper sauce (optional)	
	Rice and Peas (recipe follows)	

■ Season chicken lightly with salt, pepper and thyme; let stand for 30 minutes. In skillet, heat oil over medium-high heat; brown chicken lightly. Remove chicken and set aside.

■ Drain off all but 2 tbsp (25 mL) fat from pan. Add onion, garlic, gingerroot (if using) and curry powder; cook, stirring, for 3 minutes. Return chicken to pan; stir to coat with seasoning. Add chicken stock; cover and simmer until chicken is no longer pink inside, about 30 minutes. If desired, season with more curry powder, hot pepper sauce, and salt and pepper to taste. Serve with Rice and Peas. Makes 4 servings.

	RICE AND PEAS	
1/2 cup	small red peas (or other dried peas or beans)	125 mL
1-1/2 cups	boiling salted water	375 mL
1/2 cup	coconut milk (optional)	125 mL
1 cup	rice	250 mL
1	small onion, chopped	1
1 tbsp	butter	15 mL
1/4 tsp	dried thyme	1 mL
1/2 tsp	salt	2 mL
Pinch	pepper	Pinch

■ In saucepan, boil peas in water until tender, about 1 hour. Drain liquid into measuring cup; add coconut milk (if using), plus enough water to make 2 cups (500 mL).

■ Return liquid to peas in saucepan. Add rice, onion, butter, thyme, salt and pepper; simmer, covered, until liquid is absorbed and rice is tender, about 30 minutes. Makes 4 servings.

(centre) Caribbean Chicken with Rice and Peas ►

Stir-Fried Chicken Livers with Orange and Ginger

Serve these tasty chicken livers with brown rice and a green vegetable.

1	**sweet red or green pepper**	**1**
1	**orange**	**1**
1 tbsp	**soy sauce**	**15 mL**
1 tsp	**granulated sugar**	**5 mL**
1 tsp	**cornstarch**	**5 mL**
Dash	**hot pepper sauce**	**Dash**
3/4 lb	**chicken livers**	**375 g**
1 tbsp	**vegetable oil**	**15 mL**
1	**large onion, slivered**	**1**
1 tbsp	**minced gingerroot**	**15 mL**
1	**clove garlic, minced**	**1**
	Chopped fresh coriander or green onion	

■ Cut red pepper into 2-inch (5 cm) long strips. Using vegetable peeler, remove orange rind and cut into julienne strips; set aside.

■ Squeeze orange to make 1/3 cup (75 mL) juice; stir in soy sauce, sugar, cornstarch and hot pepper sauce. Set aside.

■ Rinse chicken livers and pat dry; remove any fat and cut into 1-inch (2.5 cm) pieces. In nonstick skillet, heat oil over high heat; stir-fry onion, gingerroot, garlic and chicken livers for 4 minutes, stirring vigorously.

■ Add orange rind and red pepper; stir-fry for 1 minute or until pepper is tender-crisp. Stir in orange juice mixture; cook, stirring, until thickened, about 1 minute. Garnish with coriander. Makes 4 servings.

Chicken Livers Creole

Chicken livers are hard to beat for value, flavor and versatility. They lend themselves to a great variety of seasonings and are very quick to cook. In fact, the most important thing to remember is to cook them briefly, just until they are no longer pink in the centre, so that they remain moist and delicious.

1/4 cup	**olive oil**	**50 mL**
1 cup	**chopped onions**	**250 mL**
1	**clove garlic, minced**	**1**
1 cup	**chopped celery**	**250 mL**
1 cup	**chopped sweet green pepper**	**250 mL**
2 cups	**canned tomatoes (with liquid)**	**500 mL**
1	**bay leaf**	**1**
1/2 tsp	**dried thyme**	**2 mL**
Dash	**hot pepper sauce (or pinch hot pepper flakes)**	**Dash**
	Salt and pepper	
2 tbsp	**vegetable oil**	**25 mL**
1 tbsp	**butter**	**15 mL**
1 lb	**chicken livers, halved if large**	**500 g**
	Hot cooked rice	

■ In large skillet or saucepan, heat olive oil over medium heat; cook onions, garlic, celery and green pepper, stirring, until softened but not browned. Add tomatoes, bay leaf, half of the thyme, hot pepper sauce, and salt and pepper to taste; reduce heat and simmer for 15 minutes. Remove bay leaf. Taste and adjust seasoning.

■ Meanwhile, in separate large skillet, heat vegetable oil with butter over medium-high heat; cook chicken livers, stirring, until browned all over but still moist inside, about 5 minutes. Combine livers and sauce. Season with remaining thyme, and salt and pepper to taste. Serve immediately over rice. Makes about 4 servings.

Credits

Recipes in THE CANADIAN LIVING COOKING COLLECTION have been created by the *Canadian Living* Test Kitchen and by the following food writers from across Canada: **Elizabeth Baird, Karen Brown, Joanna Burkhard, James Chatto, Diane Clement, David Cohlmeyer, Pam Collacott, Bonnie Baker Cowan, Pierre Dubrulle, Eileen Dwillies, Nancy Enright, Carol Ferguson, Margaret Fraser, Susan Furlan, Anita Goldberg, Barb Holland, Patricia Jamieson, Arlene Lappin, Anne Lindsay, Lispeth Lodge, Mary McGrath, Susan Mendelson, Bernard Meyer, Beth Moffatt, Rose Murray, Iris Raven, Gerry Shikatani, Jill Snider, Kay Spicer, Linda Stephen, Bonnie Stern, Lucy Waverman, Carol White, Ted Whittaker** and **Cynny Willet**.

The full-color photographs throughout are by Canada's leading food photographers, including **Fred Bird, Doug Bradshaw, Christopher Campbell, Nino D'Angelo, Frank Grant, Michael Kohn, Suzanne McCormick, Claude Noel, John Stephens** and **Mike Visser**.

Editorial and Production Staff: Hugh Brewster, Susan Barrable, Catherine Fraccaro, Wanda Nowakowska, Sandra L. Hall, Beverley Renahan and Bernice Eisenstein.

Index